A FRIEND IN THE LIBRARY

TRAVEL

BY

EVA MARCH TAPPAN

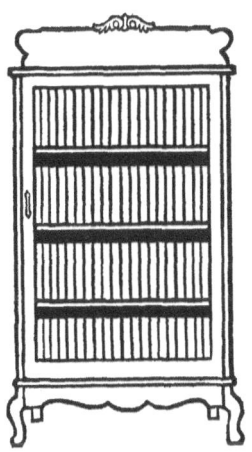

British Library Cataloguing-in-Publication Data
A catalogue record for this book is available from the
British Library

TRAVEL

A FRIEND IN THE LIBRARY

A Practical Guide to the Writings of

RALPH WALDO EMERSON

NATHANIEL HAWTHORNE

HENRY WADSWORTH LONGFELLOW

JAMES RUSSELL LOWELL

JOHN GREENLEAF WHITTIER

OLIVER WENDELL HOLMES

IN TWELVE VOLUMES

VOLUME II

Eva March Tappan

Eva March Tappan was born on 26th December 1854 in Blackstone, Massachusetts, America. She is well known as a factual as well as fictional writer, but spent her early career as a teacher. Tappan was the only child of Reverend Edmund March Tappan and Lucretia Logée, and received her education at the esteemed Vassar College. This was a private coeducational liberal arts college, in the town of Poughkeepsie, New York, from which she graduated in 1875. Here, Tappan was a member of Phi Beta Kappa, the oldest honour society for the liberal arts and sciences, widely considered as the nations most prestigious society. She also edited the *Vassar Miscellany,* a college publication.

After leaving her early education, Tappan began teaching at Wheaton College, one of the oldest institutions of higher education for women in the United States, founded in 1834 and based in Norton, Massachusetts. She taught Latin and German here, from 1875 until 1880, before moving on to the Raymond Academy in Camden, New Jersey where she was associate Principal until 1894. Tappan also received a graduate degree in English Literature from the University of Pennsylvania. This allowed her to pursue her first love, that of reading and writing, and she taught as head of the English department at the English High School at Worcester, Massachusetts.

It was only after this date that Tappan began her literary career, writing about famous characters in history, often aimed at educating children in important historical themes and epochs. Some of her better known works include, *In the Days of William the Conqueror* (1901) and *In the Days of Queen Elizabeth* (1902), *The Out-of-Door Book* (1907), *When Knights Were Bold* (1911) and *The Little Book of the Flag* (1917). Tappan never married, being a happy singleton, and died on 29th January 1930, aged seventy-five.

TRAVEL

IT once came to pass that I was requested to read some notes of travel written by a lady who had gone over an exceedingly interesting route. At the end of the manuscript, my first thought was, "How glad I am that I was not obliged to take that journey with her!" Judging by what she had written, the only places that had aroused her enthusiasm were those at which she had found well-prepared dinners, and she had passed through that delightful country with hardly a thought of its beauty or its associations. The old Roman Seneca was right when he said, more than eighteen hundred years ago, "He that would make his travels delightful must first make himself delightful." That is why traveling in books is such a pleasure. You can choose whatever route you like, and you can be sure of good company. Moreover, if the time comes when you are tired of even the best society, you can close the book without a "By your leave," and wander away into some wonderland of the imagination not mentioned in the gazetteers.

Some one ought to plan little trips in our own country and elsewhere, "personally conducted" by the best writers, trips that one could take comfortably on a stormy evening in an easy-chair in one's own library. Supposing one of them began on the Merrimac River and followed around the coast of Massachusetts. Whittier loved the Merrimac, and he will tell you what he saw on its shores ("June on the Merrimac," iv. 181): —

These banks of bloom,
The upland's wavy line,
And how the sunshine tips with fire
The needles of the pine.

A little way upstream is Lowell, Massachusetts, Whittier's "City of a Day" (v. 351). This was Lowell of the earlier times, a sort of Eldorado, an enchanted country, where a farmer's daughter might find congenial friends in her work-mates, might fill in the gaps of her education, send a shy poem or sketch to the "Lowell Offering," and at the same time be earning fabulous wages to help lift a mortgage from the home farm, or send to college a brother of ministerial inclinations, whose future career might bring honor and blessing to his family ("The Lighting Up," v. 376). Go around Cape Ann, and here is Beverly, which is, according to Lowell ("Letters," xiv. 284), "only the Bay of Naples translated into the New England dialect." Sail across the little harbor and take some walks with Hawthorne in the Salem of 1835 (xviii). See with him the gloomy water and the vessel all alight with sunshine (page 22), the scarlet barberries, the tracks of the sea birds on the beach; go with him to the Custom House where he "murdered so many of the brightest hours of the day"; or to the wharves, where he who was to become our noblest writer of romance kept tally for coal-shovelers, and incidentally noted the magnificent butterflies that haunted the place, and wondered if they were "lovely fantasies of the mind" (xviii. 283).

Then, too, there is Hawthorne's own house, to which, as he says (page 424) with good-

natured mockery and unconscious prediction,
— for those were the days before his fame had
been won, — "Pilgrims will come to pay their
tribute of reverence; they will put off their
shoes at the threshold for fear of desecrating
the tattered old carpets!" If the wind is right,
maybe you can hear the harmony of far-away
bells, Longfellow's "Curfew of the setting
sun!" ("The Bells of Lynn," iii. 143). In
Boston there is Long Wharf, where Haw-
thorne still watched the measuring of coal, and
went home to write in his journal a poetical
account of the coming of a breeze (xviii. 268).
Emerson writes ("Boston," ix. 212) of the

> Happy town beside the sea,
> Whose roads lead everywhere to all.

When you travel with poets, there are no
limitations of time or space, and Holmes will

point out Bunker Hill and tell the story of the battle, of "the bright steel glancing all along the line advancing" ("Grandmother's Story of the Bunker-Hill Battle," xiii. 149). Holmes would not be Holmes if he did not give you a bit of fun after a tale of bloodshed. He will show you the "pudding-stone" of Dorchester and tell you ("The Dorchester Giant," xii. 19) of the giant's unruly family and their plum pudding: —

> They flung it over to Roxbury hills,
> They flung it over the plain,
> And all over Milton and Dorchester too
> Great lumps of pudding the giants threw;
> They tumbled as thick as rain.

But Holmes grows serious when he writes of the Washington Elm in Cambridge ("Under the Washington Elm," xiii. 72); and well he may, for only a week before the writing of the poem, the first guns of the Civil War were fired. Lowell, too, wrote of the Elm ("Under the Old Elm," xiii. 82). He loved Cambridge. He said ("On a Certain Condescension in Foreigners," i. 293) : "I know one person who is singular enough to think Cambridge the very best spot on the habitable globe. Doubtless God could have made a better, but doubtless he never did." Lowell, in "Cambridge Thirty Years Ago," (i. 1), wrote of the Cambridge of his earlier years when "Everybody knew everybody, and all about everybody," and when the college boys who were to "have a part" at Commencement used to go to the Gravel Pit to rehearse. Lowell's commencement "part" came in 1865, twenty-seven years after his graduation, when he read his noble "Commemoration Ode" (xiii. 18), with its magnificent tribute to Abraham Lincoln.

For him her [Nature] Old-World moulds aside she
    threw,
    And, choosing sweet clay from the breast
    Of the unexhausted West,
With stuff untainted shaped a hero new,
Wise, steadfast in the strength of God, and true.

Two days before Commencement, Lowell had not written a line of this Ode, was "dull as a door-mat," he declared. Suddenly the inspiration seized him. He worked all night long, then carried the poem to his friend Child, saying, "I have something, but don't yet know what it is, or whether it will do." Child read a passage here and there, and exclaimed, "Do? I should think so! Don't you be scared."

Not far beyond Cambridge is Sudbury, the

place of the inn which Longfellow made famous in his "Tales of a Wayside Inn" (iv). Go on a little farther and you come to Concord, whose share in the first day of the Revolution Emerson has marked by his "Concord Hymn" (ix. 158).

> By the rude bridge that arched the flood,
> Their flag to April's breeze unfurled,
> Here once the embattled farmers stood
> And fired the shot heard round the world.

Return to Boston and sail along to the southward, hugging the coast, and soon you will come to the wide-mouthed bay on whose shore the half-frozen little band of Pilgrims made their home. If you have a good deal of imagination, you can picture to yourself their landing, and you can wander in fancy up the winding street where the seven little cottages stood. Then read Longfellow's "Courtship of Miles Standish" (ii. 305) for a chapter of the Pilgrim life in the earliest days of the little colony.

When one journeys in books, travel is swift, and in five minutes you can be around the arm of Cape Cod and at the island kingdom of Naushon. Holmes says of it ("The Autocrat," i. 39) : —

It is the most splendid domain that any man looks upon in these latitudes. Blue sea around it, and running up into its heart, so that the little boat slumbers like a baby in lap, while the tall ships are stripping naked to fight the hurricane outside, and storm stay-sails banging and flying in ribbons. Trees, in stretches of miles; beeches, oaks, most numerous, — many of them hung with moss, looking like bearded Druids; some coiled in the clasp of huge, dark-stemmed grapevines.

Open patches where the sun gets in and goes to sleep, and the winds come so finely sifted that they are as soft as swan's-down. Rocks scattered about, — Stonehenge-like monoliths. Fresh-water lakes; one of them, Mary's Lake, crystal-clear, full of flashing pickerel lying under the lily-pads like tigers in the jungle.

Holmes adds, "How can a man help writing poetry in such a place?" Evidently Emerson could not, for at Naushon he wrote ("Waldeinsamkeit," ix. 249): —

> I do not count the hours I spend
> In wandering by the sea;
> The forest is my loyal friend,
> Like God it useth me.

In the same group of islands as the enchanted pleasure land of Naushon is a little wind-swept isle, Penikese, now the abode of suffering and hopelessness. But here it was

that Agassiz founded his school for the study
of nature. Only a few months later, the great
teacher died. The school died with him, but
Whittier in his "Prayer of Agassiz" (ii. 295)
has saved a tender memorial of the "beautiful
white day" of its opening:—

> Said the Master to the youth:
> "We have come in search of truth,
>   Trying with uncertain key
>   Door by door of mystery;
>   We are reaching through His laws,
>   To the garment hem of Cause.
>   .   .   .   .
>
>   On the threshold of our task
>   Let us light and guidance ask,
>   Let us pause in silent prayer!"
>
> Then the Master in his place
> Bowed his head a little space,
>   And the leaves by soft airs stirred,
>   Lapse of wave and cry of bird,

Left the solemn hush unbroken
Of that wordless prayer unspoken,
While its wish, on earth unsaid,
Rose to heaven interpreted.

This is only one of the many journeys that you can take with the poets for friends and companions. You can wander through the forests of Maine with Hawthorne and Lowell, and through the Adirondacks with Emerson. You can go to the very heart of the lakes and mountains of New Hampshire and along the beautiful Bearcamp River with Whittier. Longfellow will lead you to

The narrow aisle, the bare, white wall,
The pews, and the pulpit quaint and tall

of the tiny St. David's at Radnor; or far to the westward where stands the mountain with the snowy cross upon its breast. With Hawthorne you can journey to Niagara Falls, the Falls of seventy-five years ago, approached by slow and lumbering stage-coach rather than limited express. There you will meet with him the two tradesmen who thought the canal at Lockport a far grander sight than the Falls; the "ruddy, middle-aged gentleman" who gazed at the cataract and "evinced his appro-bation by a broad grin"; the traveler who strove with earnest labor to adjust Niagara to a certain printed description; and a wanderer who evidently thought that if Nature had had *his* artistic taste, she would have changed the site of Goat Island. But there, too, is Hawthorne himself, telling frankly of the disappointment which he felt at his first sight of the Falls, — a disappointment shared by every one who loves the marvelous in nature, — and then of the " growing capacity to enjoy it," to marvel and to reverence, which comes to him who is worthy.

It is interesting to note how the different authors look upon European travel. Whittier never crossed the ocean. In more than one of his poems there is a gentle wistfulness to gaze upon the beauties and wonders of that other world; but he is always comforted by the thought that from his own doorway he can see ("The Last Walk in Autumn," ii. 37) "the miracle of flowers and trees." He says : —

> At times I long for gentler skies,
>   And bathe in dreams of softer air,
> But homesick tears would fill the eyes
>   That saw the Cross without the Bear.

Emerson admits ("Culture," vi. 129) that " for some men travel may be useful"; but he

15

is never weary of declaring that the traveler finds "only so much beauty or worth as he carries," and that "the stuff of all countries is just the same." "Do you suppose there is any country where they do not scald milk-pans, and swaddle the infants, and burn the brushwood, and broil the fish?" he queries. When Emerson crossed the Atlantic, his object was ("First Visit to England," v. 1) "to see the faces of three or four writers, — Coleridge, Wordsworth, Landor, De Quincey, and . . . Carlyle." He kept a diary of his journeyings in the good old conscientious fashion of making the most of whatever advantages came in the way; but he says that on looking it over he finds nothing about places that is worth publishing. He had, however, spent an hour with Coleridge, Wordsworth had recited poetry to him, the old lion Landor had shown him the utmost gentleness and courtesy, Carlyle had taken him to walk and had discoursed on the immortality of the soul. This walk was the beginning of a lifelong friendship between the two philosophers. Some years later Emerson paid another visit to England, whose literary result was his "English Traits" (v). He and Carlyle made an excursion together to see Stonehenge (v. 273). They counted the "uncanny stones," they walked around them and climbed over them, they listened to "the lark which was hatched last year, and the wind which was hatched many thousand years ago," as Carlyle said. Emerson took notes of the explanations and theories of the "local antiquary," then went away, "content to leave the problem with the rocks."

Hawthorne visited Stonehenge. He did not count the stones, but he looked upon them with respect, for, as he wrote ("Notes of Travel," xx. 179), "Nobody's work is likely to endure till it becomes a mystery as to who built it, and how, and for what purpose." He does not fail to note the curious life of an artist who had spent many years in the place, making sketches of the rocks to sell to visitors, "haunting Stonehenge like the ghost of a Druid."

Hawthorne went to England as consul, and has left an amusing account (xi. 1) of his consular experiences with the "beggarly and piratical-looking scoundrels" who tried to persuade him that they were Americans, and also of more agreeable details of his London life. He gives a most entertaining description of his

first after-dinner speech ("Civic Banquets,"
xi. 455), of his agonies of mind when he "be-
came sensible of a drift in his Worship's re-
marks" toward a response by the representa-
tive of the United States of America. He made
a speech "not more than two or three inches
long," and sat down, feeling, as he says, "like
a recruit who has been for the first time under
fire."

When free from consular duties, Haw-
thorne roamed about with his family in Eng-
land, Scotland, France, and Italy; and in his
"Notes of Travel" (xix–xxii) and "Our Old
Home" (xi) is the account of their journey-
ings and sight-seeings. One of the greatest
charms of these note-books is the genuineness
with which they are written. Hawthorne
never pretends an interest that he does not

feel. He writes of the Poets' Corner in West-minster Abbey (xix. 413), or of a group of girls from a charity school playing "blind-man's buff on a new plan" (xix. 309), or he gives (xix. 238) a most exquisite description of the progress of a stone wall from the laying of the bare stones to the time when it has be-come a thing of beauty with its fern and ivy and soft green moss, and "looks as if God had had at least as much to do with it as man." He notes with amusement (xx. 264) the stub-born donkey that was utterly regardless of kicks, but obeyed at once when a man called affectionately, "Come along, brother."

Hawthorne visited Abbotsford (xx. 137), and felt as if it had been made only a great museum; but of the room where Scott died, he says, "it seemed to me that we spoke with a sort of hush in our voices, as if he were still dying there, or had but just departed." In Italy Hawthorne is rather whimsically — or wearily — rejoiced when he finds in a certain palace that there are few pictures which he need look at; but the pictures that please him he visits over and over again. In his early sketch of a visit to Niagara, he wrote that there were moments when, as he gazed at the Falls, there seemed to be nothing in the world save himself and the river. So when he stands before the perfection of the Apollo Belvidere, he says, "I saw the Apollo Belvidere as something ethereal and godlike; only for a flitting moment, however, and as if he had alighted from heaven, or shone suddenly out of the sunshine, and then had withdrawn himself again" (xxi. 268). So it is that Hawthorne writes of his travels, always genuine and always with something of his own to add to his description, the thoughts and fancies that the place or the thing brings to his mind. He is more than a friendly traveling companion, he is the wielder of some magic wand by which he permits us to look upon scenes and people through the eyes of the master of romance.

Holmes went abroad as a young man to study medicine. He carried notes of introduction to two men in England, one of whom invited him to dinner, the other to tea. He spent most of his time in Paris, but made various tours, one to Stratford-on-Avon, concerning which he says, "Emotions, but no scribbling of name on walls." Half a century later, he went abroad again; to his own surprise, he declares. He expected "a little rest," but he was no longer an unknown medical student; he was the famous "Autocrat." Every one wanted to welcome him and entertain him. The biddings to dinner and tea expanded into hundreds of invitations, which began to be cabled across the Atlantic as soon as it was known that he was coming. He was taken to Cambridge, where he received his "formal sentence as Doctor of Letters" ("Our Hundred Days in Europe," x. 76), and where the undergraduates cried, "A speech! a speech! Holmes, sweet Holmes!" a play on his name which he admitted was "not absolutely a novelty" to his ears. The University of Edinburgh gave him another degree, and Oxford gave him still another, while the students in the gallery shouted, "Did he come in the One-Hoss Shay?" At Oxford he put a tape measure around one of the stately old elms, or, as he calls the action in "The Autocrat" (i. 230), put his wedding ring on it, and was just a bit jealous of Old England when he found that the tree needed a longer line than any of his "tree-wives" in New England.

This much belettered man visited rambling old country mansions with "every accommodation for a spiritual visitant," and was rather aggrieved that no haunted chamber or ineradicable bloodstain was shown him. He met a noted surgeon, and went home to question which would give the more satisfaction to a thoroughly humane and unselfish being, to have written all the plays of Shakespeare, or to have saved from death by medical skill some seven score of suffering women. Holmes's daughter recorded that on the summit of a

certain mountain her honored parent nearly
blew away; but the honored parent declared
that as two young men near him were exposed
to the fury of the wind, he offered an arm to
each, which they were not too proud to accept.
He had some shoes made in England, but
could not express his feelings about them with-
out "dangerously enlarging" his vocabulary.
He wandered about the places in Paris that
he had known in his student days. Then he
went back to England, to meet again what
he called a "constantly changing agreeable
companionship." He says that the conversa-
tion usually began : —

"It is a very long time since you have been
in this country, I believe?"

"It is a *very* long time: fifty years and
more."

"You find great changes in London, of course, I suppose?"

So it began, but it was almost certain to lead to pleasant talk, never heated or noisy and always of interest. The bitterest politician that Holmes met, so he declares, was a dog "who refused a desirable morsel offered him in the name of Mr. Gladstone, but snapped up another instantly on being told that it came from Queen Victoria."

Holmes returned to Boston, to write his book, but in it to warn the "gentle readers" that he had given only first impressions, and that they must beware of hasty conclusions. "If a foreigner of limited intelligence were whirled through England on the railways," he says, "he would naturally come to the conclusion that the chief product of that country is

mustard, and that its most celebrated people
are Mr. Keen and Mr. Colman, whose great
advertising boards, yellow letters on a black
ground, and black letters on a yellow ground,
stare the traveler in the face at every station."
So speaks Holmes, and what a man says who
has been lettered by three universities within
three months must be true.

When Hawthorne was in Liverpool, in
1854, he wrote to Longfellow, "Why don't you
come over, being now a man of leisure and
with nothing to keep you in America? If I
were in your position, I think I should make
my home on this side of the water, — though
always with an indefinite and never-to-be-
executed intention to go back and die in my
native land." Longfellow had made his first
trip to Europe a quarter of a century earlier,

when he, a young graduate of eighteen, was offered the professorship of modern languages at his Alma Mater. He went abroad for three years to study, and also to write the sketches which afterwards appeared in book form as "Outre-Mer" (vii). This is a collection of vivid descriptions of people and places, legends, charming bits of literary talk, and an occasional translation. He could hardly believe that his dreams of travel had come true, and he wandered along the River Loire on foot, or "rattled on like an earthquake" in the diligence on the road to Spain, with a halo of youth and happiness and talent around him. He visited a quaint little Spanish village where the people "kept every saint's day in the calendar, and devoutly hung Judas once a year in effigy." He avowed himself a disap-

pointed man in that he had bought a watch
"large enough for the clock of a village
church," for the express purpose of having it
stolen by a highwayman, but had met with no
such longed-for experience. He came across
one man who boasted of the little he had seen
in much journeying, and another who boasted
of the vast amount *he* had seen in almost no
time at all. He dropped a coin into a beggar's
hat, and resolved for the future "not to take
for a beggar every poor gentleman who chose
to stand in the shade with his hat in his hand
on a hot summer's day."

A few years later Longfellow wrote "Hype-
rion" (viii), a book of European wanderings, a
romance, but with only a thread of story. The
special charm of the book is that it expresses
the poet's own feelings. It gives several of his

translations — and no one else can catch the spirit of a foreign writer so perfectly as he. Here is his "I know a maiden fair to see" (224), and "Hast thou seen that lordly castle?" (212). Here is his exquisite description of the Rhone glacier (174), ending, "Its shape is that of a glove, lying with the palm downwards, and the fingers crooked and close together. It is a gauntlet of ice, which, centuries ago, Winter, the king of these mountains, threw down in defiance to the Sun; and year by year the Sun strives in vain to lift it from the ground on the point of his glittering spear" (174). Many years after his first visit to Europe, Longfellow wrote his sonnet to Venice (iii. 230): —

White swan of cities, slumbering in thy nest
So wonderfully built among the reeds

Of the lagoon, that fences thee and feeds,
As sayeth thy old historian and thy guest!

"The ancient town of Bruges" touched his fancy as with magic. He wandered about the streets, "and felt myself a hundred years old," he said. "Oh, those chimes, those chimes!" he wrote in his diary, "how deliciously they lull one to sleep! The little bells, with their clear, liquid notes, like the voices of boys in a choir, and the solemn bass of the great bell tolling in, like the voice of a friar!" (i. 205). "The Belfry of Bruges and Other Poems" he named one of his volumes (i. 207). Beautiful Amalfi, too, had great charm for him, and of this bewitching city he wrote ("Amalfi," iii. 92): —

Sweet the memory is to me
Of a land beyond the sea,

Where the waves and mountains meet,
Where, amid her mulberry trees,
Sits Amalfi in the heat,
Bathing ever her white feet
In the tideless summer seas.

On one of Lowell's earliest journeys, he
went by rail to his namesake city at the terrific
speed of twenty miles an hour. Railroads
were novelties in those days. One was pro-
posed between Boston and Portsmouth, but
this boy of sixteen wrote that there was not
trade enough between the two cities to sup-
port a road, and he doubted whether any rail-
roads would be profitable. After the novelty
had worn off, he said profoundly (xiv. 12),
"the passenger cars would not be so full."
When, in later years, he went abroad, he de-
clared that he fled to Europe to escape the
tyranny of his old servant. Wherever he goes,

he is the same witty, earnest, scholarly, fun-loving Lowell. He is glad when he finds in a place "no antiquities" which his conscience would require him to examine; he gives a most charming description of the annual illumination of St. Peter's (i. 236), and another equally good of an impertinent rook that busied itself gazing down the flues of the Whitby chimneys, to see what people were going to have for breakfast (xvi. 247). Lowell loved Whitby and spent many summers there. He writes of it (xvi. 242): "Whitby is a place that won't let you have a moment to yourself. . . . And while one is here, everybody expects letters from one because one has nothing to do — as if that did n't make it all the harder to do anything else." On his first visit to Europe, in 1855, he studied like a learned pig, he said; but he found time to meet some people worth knowing. Thackeray gave him and two others a dinner, which by some misapprehension had been ordered for two only (xiv. 314). Lowell says: "There were some cutlets which *did* look rather small. 'Eat one of 'em, Story,' said he [Thackeray]; 'it will make you feel a little hungry at first, but you'll *soon* get over it.' The benevolent tone he gave to the *soon* was delightfully comic."

Lowell was as ready as a small boy to enjoy any "sights." While he was minister to England he wrote to a friend (xvi. 117): —

I have one bit of secret intelligence. His Excellency and Mrs. Lowell are going to see the Lord Mayor's Show to-morrow for the first time! Don't you envy us? Real camels and real elephants, with men atop of them, and Queen Bess in all her glory! I mean to be ten years old for the nonce. Generally I am younger.

So it is that one can journey with the best of guides, guides who enjoy everything to the full, who are never wearisome, who never point out beauties to us, but let us look through their eyes and share in their pleasure. He who has books and an hour of leisure may wander whithersoever he will, and everywhere he will find beside him these ideal companions, who never intrude, but are always ready to give him of their best.

ADDITIONAL

EMERSON

Boston, xii. 181.
English Traits, v.
Monadnoc, ix. 60.
Musketaquid, ix. 141.
Boston Hymn, ix. 201.
Written at Rome, ix. 396.

HAWTHORNE

Our Old Home, xi.
An Ontario Steamboat, xvii. 209.
Sketches from Memory, xvii. 281.
American Note-Books, xviii.
Notes of Travel, xix–xxii.

HOLMES

My Hunt for "The Captain," viii. 1.
Our Hundred Days in Europe, x.
Lexington, xii. 67.
The Hudson, xii. 231.
Boston Common: Three Pictures, xii. 276.
Old Cambridge, xiii. 170.

TRAVEL

LONGFELLOW

The Beleaguered City, i. 29.
The Wreck of the Hesperus, i. 69.
The Village Blacksmith, i. 72.
The Discoverer of the North Cape, iii. 52.
Travels by the Fireside, iii. 85.
To the River Charles, i. 80.
The Arsenal at Springfield, i. 217.
Nuremberg, i. 219.
The Bridge, i. 241.
Evangeline, ii. 17.
Hiawatha, ii. 123.
The Phantom Ship, iii. 18.
In the Churchyard at Cambridge, iii. 25.
The Jewish Cemetery at Newport, iii. 31.
Songo River, iii. 99.
The Herons of Elmwood, iii. 102.
The Old Bridge at Florence, iii. 226.
In the Churchyard at Tarrytown, iii. 228.
To the River Rhone, iii. 233.
Boston, iii. 237.
St. John's, Cambridge, iii. 237.
Woodstock Park, iii. 239.

The Cross of Snow, iii. 242.
Mad River, iii. 323.
The Bells of San Blas, iii. 328.

LOWELL

A Moosehead Journal, i. 69.
Leaves from My Journal in Italy and Else-where, i. 119.
Pictures from Appledore, xii. 201.
Letters, xiv–xvi.

WHITTIER

The Angels of Buena Vista, i. 112.
The Garrison of Cape Ann, i. 166.
Skipper Ireson's Ride, i. 174.
The Pipes at Lucknow, i. 183.
The Swan Song of Parson Avery, i. 188.
The Double-Headed Snake of Newbury, i. 192.
The Red River Voyageur, i. 215.
Among the Hills, i. 260.
In the "Old South," i. 371.
The Rock-Tomb of Bradore, i. 388.
The Bay of Seven Islands, i. 390.

QUESTIONS

1. What is the best rule for the enjoyment of travel?

   Seneca's, "He who would make his travels delightful must first make himself delightful."

2. Where is the most beautiful tribute to Lincoln to be found?

In Lowell's "Commemoration Ode" (xiii. 18).

3. In what qualities does the excellence of this tribute consist?

In a poetical expression of a thoroughly sympathetic appreciation of Lincoln's character and greatness.

4. Who are the characters in the "Tales of a Wayside Inn" (iv)?

Musician	*Ole Bull*
Poet	*T. W. Parsons*
Spanish Jew	*Israel Edrehi*
Sicilian	*Luigi Monti*
Theologian	*Daniel Treadwell*
Student	*Henry Ware Wales*

5. Which of these Tales have an American foundation?

"Paul Revere's Ride."
"The Birds of Killingworth."
"Lady Wentworth."

"Elizabeth."

"The Rhyme of Sir Christopher."

6. Who wrote the first English book containing a collection of stories purporting to be told by a group of people?
   Chaucer, in his "Canterbury Tales."

7. Which is the most famous line in Emerson's "Concord Hymn" (ix. 158)?
   The fourth, because it expresses so much in so few words.

8. Which two poets have written most about America?
   Whittier and Longfellow.

8. What does Emerson regard as the "best fruit of travel"?
   Conversation (vi. 269).

9. What is the special charm of Hawthorne's description of his travels?
   The revelation of his own fancies and dreams.

10. What is the special charm of Longfellow's description of places?

His poetic thought.

11. Wherein lies the charm of Lowell's letters on his travels?

In his wit and humor.

12. What is the special charm of Holmes's "Our Hundred Days in Europe" (x)?

His frank egoism.

13. Why is "Outre-Mer" (vii) a remarkable book for a young man to write?

Because of the smoothness and finish of its style.

14. Why are Longfellow's translations especially good?

Because they are exceedingly literal and poetical, and catch the spirit of their originals.

15. What is one of the special beauties of Longfellow's poems?

Their similes.

16. In Whittier's "Tent on the Beach" (iv. 227), who are his companions?
    James T. Fields and Bayard Taylor.

17. Which of the twelve poems are on foreign subjects?
    "The Brother of Mercy" and "Kallundborg Church."

www.ingramcontent.com/pod-product-compliance
Lightning Source LLC
Chambersburg PA
CBHW020919180626
46816CB00007BA/2484